TORONTO

BORIS SPREMO
and his camera
look at

TORONTO

McGRAW-HILL COMPANY OF CANADA LIMITED

| Toronto | New York | London |
| Sydney | Johannesburg | Mexico |

TORONTO

Library of Congress Catalog Card Number 67-20721

1 2 3 4 5 6 7 8 9 LP-67 9 8 7

Printed and bound in Canada

The text by

DOROTHY
JANE
GOULDING

What gives a big city its character? Why is Paris thought of as a city for lovers, London a mecca for literary men, Cairo a symbol of mystery and adventure? What, in short, is in a name?

The name, Toronto, implies a mass of contradictions. To some it is a thriving modern city, with its own harbour, airport, cultural centres, high accident record, and shifting population, indistinguishable from countless other modern cities around the world. To others it is a backwash of conservatism, Hog Town well named, a city of churches, the biggest small town on the continent, Muddy York, or the only cemetery with streetcars running through it. In the search for the true character of this suddenly grown cosmopolitan city, there are all these contrasts to be considered.

The origin of the name itself is a subject of controversy. The site of several Indian settlements during the sixteenth century, it was in a strategic position, lying as it did at the junction of the trade route between Lakes Huron and Ontario with the trail along the north shore from Montreal to the Mississippi. The name, Teiaigon, of the Seneca village located at the gateway to the Huron region was translated variously as Place of Meeting, Trees in the Water, Between the Lakes, and Lake Opening. Perhaps the city derived its present name from Tarantou, which first appears on a map of 1656, and has been applied at different times to the whole area between Lake Simcoe and Lake Ontario, the north portage at Lake Simcoe, the settlement at the mouth of the Humber, and the present city. There was also a great Huron chief who lived in the Lake Simcoe area, called Daronto. The settlement might have been named for him.

It is generally agreed, however, that the first white man to see the north shore of Lake Ontario, and thus to set foot on the site of the future city, was Etienne Brûlé. He was a young man who came to Canada with Champlain in 1608, spent two years with the Indians, and was sent by his commander to enlist the help of Indian tribes against the English, the Dutch, and the hostile Iroquois. A plaque at the corner of Weston and Clouston Roads in Mount Dennis records this bit of history. However, Toronto showed scant respect for its first Great White Father. European politics and Indian wars resulted in the burning of all the Huron villages along the north shore, and Brûlé so lost face with his adopted brothers that he is believed to have been killed by them, then eaten. Torontonians, though still lacking a reputation for open-hearted friendliness to strangers, have improved in the past three hundred years!

Old Fort York, substantially the same today as it was during the War of 1812, cannon at the ready to repulse the Menace from the United States.

By 1690, Teiaigon had come under Mississauga control, and in the early eighteenth century, with the power of the Iroquois broken under Frontenac's firm rule, the French fortified a trading post at Fort Niagara and a subsidiary one at Toronto, Le Poste du Fond du Lac. There is some evidence that a Sulpician centre had been founded some years previously, but little is known of it. When the English built a fort at Oswego in competition with the French, La Jonquiere ordered a large fort built at the foot of the Humber River. Completed in 1750, it was called Fort Toronto. True to the city's later tradition, it was found inadequate before it was completed, and a bigger fort was built in the next two years at the foot of what is now Dufferin Street. This one was officially called Fort Rouillé, but was still known as Fort Toronto. In 1759 it was burned by the French to prevent its use by the English.

Canada was now in the hands of the British and proved a haven of refuge for those of the United Empire Loyalists who managed to escape the "horrors of democracy" by fleeing across the border. Many settled in southern Ontario, and when in 1787

2

the British acquired a large tract of land from the Mississaugas in what came to be known as the Toronto Purchase, the tiny colony began to grow. About one-third of the present York County was bought for 1,700 pounds in cash and merchandise, a substantial part being firewater. Hardly an auspicious beginning for a future staunch centre of blue-law morality, but it is not every investment that turns out to be worth thousands of times its original cost.

Four years later the country was divided into Lower and Upper Canada, and in 1797 Sir John Graves Simcoe was sent out as the first Lieutenant-Governor of the new province. His wife was an excellent correspondent and kept a faithful diary of her experiences in this new situation. It is thanks to her feminine attention to insignificant detail that we know as much as we do about the first years of the town. Simcoe rechristened the garrison York in honour of the Duke of York, son of George III, who had recently been made Commander-in-Chief of the army, despite a lamentable lack of success on the continent against the French. Perhaps it was in York that the famous rhyme was first chanted:

> The Grand old Duke of York,
> He had ten thousand men;
> He marched them up to the top of the hill,
> Then he marched them down again.

Simcoe planned the town on aristocratic principles, laying out the blocks with certain streets reserved for tradesmen and others of their class, and began a program of roadbuilding.

The Parliament Buildings, home of the Legislature of the Province of Ontario.

When relations with the United States grew more strained, it was he who was instrumental in moving the seat of government from Niagara to York, which he felt could be more easily defended. Despite this precaution, in 1813 American ships landed west of Fort York, and when the defenders had moved hurriedly eastward, the soldiers stormed the garrison. A magazine exploded killing over two hundred Americans, and the survivors burned the legislative buildings, the library, and all the historical documents of Upper Canada, removing with them the mace, insignia of the Crown. The British, in retaliation, burned much of Washington, but the mace was not returned until 1934, when President Roosevelt made the historic gesture to mark the centennial of the founding of Toronto.

After its brief hour of military glory, York settled down to the solid virtues of growth and expansion. In 1812 its population was a scant 800. By 1817 it was considered large enough to be granted self-government, and by 1834, with a population of 10,000, it was incorporated as a city and renamed Toronto. William Lyon Mackenzie, its first mayor, established a precedent no later holder of that office was able to emulate. Within three years of his election to office, the ex-mayor was leading a troop of rebels against his former seat of honour. As a political move it was disastrous, but as a publicity gesture it has yet to be equalled! No mayor in the history of the city is apt to be remembered as well as Mackenzie, one of the leaders in the struggle for responsible government.

Despite Mackenzie's efforts to stir the town, Toronto remained peaceful, the rebels were dispersed, and the urge to violence that always seemed present in the breasts of the respectable inhabitants was channelled into the lawful spectacle of two men, Samuel Lount and Peter Mathews, being hanged in one of the best-attended public executions of the time.

The increase in influence and size that had continued for some thirty years came to an abrupt halt in 1841, when the capital was moved to Kingston. Fortunately, within eight years it was moved back again, and when Confederation was made fact, Toronto was the natural choice to be capital of Ontario. It was then that Toronto began to assume its present shape.

During the next fifty years it overflowed and annexed close to thirty communities, and its growth, delayed by two world wars and a depression, culminated in the Metropolitan Toronto Act of 1953, by which the City of Toronto and its twelve suburbs were constituted into one metropolitan municipality, the first of its kind in the western hemisphere. Toronto's "Metro experiment" is still evolving — in 1966 it entered phase two, with the transformation of its original thirteen units into six boroughs. Toronto's rate of expansion has shown no signs of abating. Already one of North America's largest cities, it is expected that by the end of the century its population will be at least four million.

*Toronto's skyline, as most Torontonians know it . . . the familiar
silhouettes of the Royal York and the Canadian Imperial Bank
of Commerce building; the Toronto-Dominion Centre, new
but already an integral part of the skyline . . . viewed
from Centre Island.*

But there are other aspects of the skyline you can't see from the Island . . .

The old City Hall tower, surprisingly overshadowed by an anonymous black chimney . . .

A bit of Olde England, the St. Lawrence Market tower, built in 1851, seen above a welter of nearby rooftops . . .

The City Hall . . .

A bit of Olde Kiev, the Ukrainian Orthodox Church on Ossington Avenue . . .

Park Towers at Walmer Road and St. Clair, framed in a Gothic arch . . .

A partial eclipse of the afternoon sun . . . the Canadian National Exhibition ferris wheel . . .

. . . and the turrets of Casa Loma.

Once there was a homely street called Yorkville, whose drab, brown dwellings were for years overshadowed by the chic, glittering shops of its glamorous neighbour, Bloor Street. Then overnight it seemed the sombre old homes were transformed, blossoming into multi-hued boutiques and coffee houses, and Yorkville became the Village, still with the old name, but now definitely where the action is. On University Avenue, right, another dramatic change, as successive styles of architecture rise above their predecessors.

When a city sprawls outward, it seems inevitable that there will follow an outbreak of shopping plazas and the network of expressways. Left, the Don Valley Parkway loops through rolling grassland and forests of apartments. And a railway track on the waterfront snakes its way among the stanchions of the Gardiner Expressway.

Full of surprises, Toronto is an explorer's
delight. Above, Pioneer Village at Steeles
Avenue and Jane Street. The Laskay Emporium,
as well as being a general store, has a small
print shop that turns out the Village newspaper.

A Russian submarine in Toronto harbour? The
ice-encrusted ferry bumpers at Centre Island
pier menace an unsuspecting city.

Some of Toronto's permanent residents: Occupying the centre of the park at St. Clair and Avenue Road, Peter Pan, a twin to the bronze boy in London's Kensington Garden; Queen Victoria, who holds court, naturally, in Queen's Park; a sombre Sibelius, immortalized in the park named for him on Bernard Avenue; and the irreverent, ubiquitous sparrow.

At the corner of Front and Wellington Streets, the old buildings have been razed to make way for parking lots. Just one remains, a familiar wedge-shaped landmark, the Gooderham Building.

A City of Change

One of the most interesting facets in the life of a city is the way an area changes from decade to decade. The street that is considered a symbol of success in twenty years may be despised as old-fashioned. Thirty years later it has fallen into rapid decay and may require a tremendous outlay of capital to be made serviceable. Such an area is Jarvis Street, which in the 1850's was a centre of fashionable living, and within a hundred years has travelled the full circle. From select residential district, it gradually drifted into genteel poverty, second-string boarding homes, and finally knew the degradation of red-light district and flop houses. Rescued from this dismal state by wholesale demolition and rebuilding, it is now the site of modern office buildings, high-rise apartments, and is itself a main traffic artery.

Toronto has been much criticised for the wholesale destruction of its past. Many of the demolished buildings were worth saving as examples of architecture in days when privilege of class gave financial support for the running of eighteen-room mansions, private conservatories, drawing rooms filled with potted palms and bric-a-brac, and halls lit by stained glass. There are still some of these homes left, but they are rare. Automatic appliances are not available to dust carved bannisters, nor is there a supply of help to chase after small children through winding passages. The modern inheritor of great-grandmother's elegance counts himself lucky to sell to an agent, who calls in the wrecking crew, demolishes the Edwardian relic, and erects a plaster and chrome substitute to house, not one, but two hundred families.

Some areas, thanks to fortuitous original design, lend themselves to discovery by the "artistic". Balconies and porches, once the badge of gentility, are ruthlessly stripped away; plaster is slapped over brick (or brick revealed from under plaster) ; paint is lavishly applied in fashionable shades of mud-brown, gunmetal-grey, or white-white; grille-work is "picked out" in green or black, and for the price of a new house, a genuine piece of Old Toronto is preserved for the young (and solvent) bohemian. Some of these rehabilitations are surprisingly effective, although surely a far cry from the original designers' intent. No matter! A street rebuilt in this way is infinitely more attractive than a row of prefabricated clapboard.

Some old buildings have been preserved as museums, such as the William Lyon Mackenzie House. Others are used by societies or institutions till funds are available for the building of modern and efficient premises. The University of Toronto has taken over many of the old homes on St. George Street as fraternity houses and graduate residences. Some old homes have been successfully subdivided into duplexes or triplexes, where zoning has permitted, and still others are serving as offices for professional men.

It was prophesied many years ago that Toronto would never develop into a major city because of its topography, which included many ravines and a lakefront. And indeed, for several years the Don Valley on the east and the Humber on the west marked the extent of the town's growth, and the push north-wards was hampered by mud and swamp and by more ravine "trouble" on Yonge Street near Hogg's Hollow.

Mrs. Anna Jameson wrote scathingly of the town of York. Lady Simcoe, kinder in her outlook, still suffered from the heat, the cold, insects, and dampness. Indeed, she buried one of her children in York. Sufferers from malaria and ague often travelled to Newark (Niagara-on-the-Lake) to recuperate. Toronto still has a climate requiring patience and fortitude, varying as it does from extreme cold to blazing heat, and for months hovering at a damp and chilling 32°. Even with air conditioning and central heating it can be difficult, and we can but admire the endurance of the early citizens.

When Governor Simcoe laid out the streets in blocks covering thirty acres, the buildings were concentrated along the waterfront, and lands north towards Bloor Street were granted to government officials and friends. The whole township was surveyed into farm lots, and much of the uninteresting street plan of today results from city thoroughfares following original concession lines. Only in larger areas such as Rosedale, the Jarvis estate, Lawrence Park (joint farms owned by the

HELP US KEEP OUR PARKS CLEAN AND TIDY

Lawrence brothers), or Forest Hill (country home of the Baldwins) have the roads taken scenic curves. Old Forest Hill Road, for instance, was originally called Trespasser's Road, since it was the trail used by Indians hunting across the Baldwin estate. Weston Road was also an Indian trail, winding northwest from Fort York. Davenport and Kingston Roads mark the shores created by the old Lake Iroquois of glacial times.

Roads were a prime necessity, but the marshy ground, underground streams, lack of labour, and public apathy combined to defeat the most progressive citizens. Jesse Ketchum used a thick coating of tanbark on the footpaths near his home and tanning factory, and pathmasters were appointed to keep the citizens alert to responsibility. Each lot owner was responsible for the road bordering his property, but mud was the enemy of

transportation most of the year, except when winter made the
use of sleighs possible. Simcoe, with his dream of York as a strong
garrison, constructed Yonge Street as a military highway and
set aside the land between Parliament and the Don River as a
naval reserve. Yonge Street was never more than a trade route,
and the land along the river, known as "The Park", blocked
eastern expansion for many years.

Yonge Street in 1796 stretched thirty-four miles from York to
Holland Landing, but keeping the new road in repair was
too great a task. Thirty years later it was still a day's journey
from York to what is now North Toronto and back, since the
only route was across the Don at Queen Street, north on
Don Mills Road, and back along the Base Line, as Eglinton was
called. In the '40's teams of oxen were still required to haul
wagons out of the mudholes north of Queen Street.

The Stump Act required lawbreakers to work at removing
stumps from the town streets. Toll gates were introduced in the
'20's, and the revenue put towards road maintenance. A rough
type of flagging was first used, then wooden planks, and a simple
type of macadamizing. Broken stones piled to the centre of the

streets and kicked by horse traffic to the sides made convenient ammunition for riots during parades and election campaigns. The speed limit was set in a charmingly vague way; vehicles were not to be driven "at an unreasonable rate", and the early parking limit was twenty-four hours.

Cabs appeared in the '30's, horse-drawn omnibuses in the '40's, and in 1861 came the horse railway — the first street railway system in Canada. The company laid cedar blocks along the routes it served, and in case of fire the cars were hastily lifted off the tracks to allow a free passage to the fire engines. As the city grew, the need for improved streets and transportation increased, and early attempts at paving with cement were tried in the '80's. By the turn of the century, both brick and asphalt streets were common, and some of the former were still in use just a few years ago.

After the first two decades of the nineteenth century, when the planning of the town was under government control, a reaction set in. Individual citizens built where and how they chose, and unfortunately money talked louder than foresight. The waterfront, which had been planned as a scenic Esplanade, gradually succumbed to the railways, till only a small stretch was left as a pleasure ground, known for years as Sunnyside. Because of the easy, low grades, ravines were natural beds for railroads. Brickyards grew up over deposits of shale; Ashbridges Bay, once a haven for fishermen, was filled in; and the Island, formerly the Peninsula until the wind and waves broke through in the '50's, became the only refuge left for those who longed for fresh air. Toronto grew north, east, and west, annexing as it went, till it developed the T-shape it held for so long.

Many of the districts acquired this way still keep their original names. Yorkville Village, now a haven for coffee-house addicts, exclusive boutiques, and cellar art, was one of the first to be taken over. In another move, the district northwest of Bloor and Avenue Road was dubbed The Annex. Cabbagetown was named for the Irish, who arrived in droves during the potato famines and dug up their front lawns to plant food, which spelled security. The Ward, an early political division, was made up of refugees from a dozen European countries, fleeing war, famine, and persecution, till in 1911 it numbered 10,000, seventy per cent of whom were Jewish. Moss Park was so called because of its marshy ground. Rosedale was named by Mary Jarvis, when she began housekeeping in her father-in-law's country home.

The first electric streetcar was demonstrated at the Exhibition of '83, but transportation was still inefficient, and the boom time encouraged land speculators to invest in the Belt Line, which was the first effort at rapid transit in Canada. The eastern leg of the route was finished in time to carry the dignitaries to the opening of the new Upper Canada College in 1892, but two years later, despite low fares and quick service (fairly quick, that is — one hour and ten minutes for a round trip of sixteen miles), lack of support forced it to be abandoned. Electricity at last took over public transportation in 1894, when the horsecars were removed. It took five years of agitation before Sunday streetcars were allowed, and even then there was much headshaking over the ungodly ways of those who sought pleasure on the Sabbath.

The Street Railway Company changed hands in 1891, and for the next thirty years there was difficulty over extending service to

Suburbia . . . thousands and thousands of identical dwellings, their sameness redeemed by the fanciful, free-flowing curves of the streets.

such outlying areas as Danforth, St. Clair, and Bloor Street West.
The city ran these independent lines, and many people
remember the old cars, with hooks on the outside where
mothers hung baby carriages before climbing aboard. The
manager, R. J. Fleming, was an ardent lacrosse fan, and anyone
carrying a lacrosse stick rode free on the Company cars. There
was excitement, too, over the strikes, and in 1902 the cars,
operated by scabs, were pelted with eggs by the strikers, who won
a wage settlement of no less than fifteen cents an hour.

When war broke out in 1914, building expansion all but
ground to a halt, with one notable exception. The Bloor Street
viaduct, "the bridge to nowhere", was built during the war years.
People decried the waste of the $2,000,000 it cost, but it brought
prosperity to "The Danforth", and foreshadowed the days
when Toronto would be linked by many such viaducts, refuting
the prophecy that ravines would impede its growth.

Today the Street Railway is run by the Transit
Commission, and streetcars are being superseded by trolley buses,
subways, and motorbuses. Streets are kept clean and in good
repair; garbage is gathered regularly; night travel is made easy by

Built in Toronto and named for a former mayor, The Sam McBride, *above, has been serving Island-bound Torontonians since 1939. Other ferries — the* William Inglis *(1935) and the* Thomas Rennie *(1951). Left, moonlight on Lake Ontario and Exhibition Park.*

efficient streetlights; and the police and fire departments have the most modern equipment at their disposal. Gone are some past pleasures, such as scribbling on the sidewalk with burned-out carbons from the incandescent streetlamps. But gone, too, are the days when living on the outskirts of the city meant virtual isolation. Don Mills, Scarborough, Downsview, and Willowdale have many residents who commute to the business section downtown every day as a matter of course.

The building of the new City Hall, to replace the 1899 version, and Nathan Phillips Square surrounding it have given new life to a section of the city which had deteriorated to a slum area. Its conception, which includes an ornamental pool that converts to a skating rink in the winter, has helped to destroy the legend of the city's unimaginative ugliness. In typical Toronto fashion, the

University Avenue through an archway at Queen's Park, left, and Scarborough Bluffs, by night.

building created a storm of controversy, equalled only by the uproar over the fate of the old City Hall, long recognized as one of the outstanding remnants of Toronto of the '90's. Now it is a rallying point for the Save-our-dear-old-Toronto brigade.

With the O'Keefe Centre, the projected St. Lawrence Centre, and the Toronto-Dominion Centre, the future of downtown Toronto looks bright. As for the suburbs, the shopping plazas, libraries, public buildings, and recreational facilities make them miniature cities in themselves. As growth continues, naturally more problems arise. Areas such as Regent's Park are remodelled along modern slum clearance lines, while future slums are built in new development areas, where acres of jerry-built homes are slapped on arid, treeless plains, with landscaping, shopping plazas, and perhaps even trips to the moon thrown in on the never-never plan. Politicians continue to play politics, editors go on publishing their own editorials, government contracts still create the odd scandal. Commuters curse the weather, the Commission, and their fellow sufferers, indiscriminately. Deputations from the Women's League, the Home and School, or Societies for the Prevention of a Dozen Things wait patiently outside the doors of City Hall officials, hoping they have found the right one. Toronto is a big city now, and these things are all part of big-city living.

31

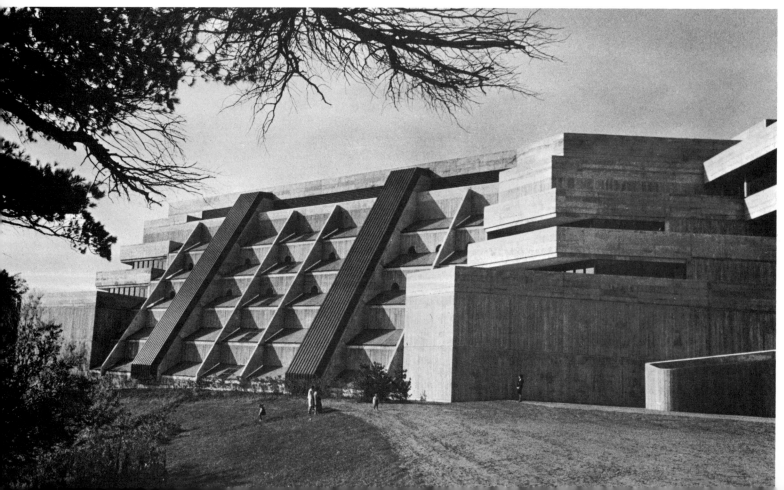

*A melange of architecture.
Top left, the Gothic spire of
St. Basil's Church and
St. Michael's College. Bottom
left, a truncated pyramid in
suburbia, Scarborough College.
The street above could be any
one of a hundred in Toronto —
rows of semi-detacheds, pillars
and porches, pocket-sized yards.
This one happens to be
Christie Street.*

University College of the University of
Toronto was built in the mid-nineteenth
century, partially gutted by fire in 1890,
then restored. Left, students saunter
through the sunlit cloister. Below, the
sweeping curves of City Hall, surely one
of the most photogenic buildings in the
the world.

One of the tree-lined streets for which Toronto is famous, at left, Pembroke Street in winter. Right, the bewildering maze of the Spadina Interchange, where traffic is channelled over and under twenty-seven bridges.

Above, Yorkville Avenue on a
spring evening — haven for hippies.
Mother and baby, right, take a
breather at the fountain
of the municipal courthouse,
University Avenue.

Two studies in speed — the
C.N.E. Flyer and the Bloor
subway (from the driver's seat).

Traffic is the inescapable bugaboo of big-city living, whether it be speeding along the curves of an expressway, crawling up a midtown hill, inching through the slush of a residential street, or crammed, sardine-style, into a parking lot. New roads and parking areas are continually being built, but relief is not yet in sight for Toronto. Opposite is the Gardiner Expressway; above, Avenue Road.

Refuge from the frantic pace of downtown — Toronto's parks. This page, High Park, almost a square mile of woods and ponds. Opposite, Alexander Muir Memorial Gardens on north Yonge, named for the composer of The Maple Leaf Forever.

A plague to pedestrians, a curse on car-owners, winter adds unique beauty to our parks. The greenbelt becomes white in Edwards Gardens, below. Right, stiff poplar skeletons bear the brunt of icy winds off Lake Ontario.

Even in the heart of this city one finds countless pockets of unusual charm — all the more prized because they are unexpected. Below, shadows from a wrought-iron railing in Rosedale transform sunlit concrete into old-fashioned embroidery; lamplight muted by falling snow in Queen's Park; opposite, moonlight lends a melancholy beauty to Jarvis Street.

Two City Halls, one old, one new, both centres of controversy — political and architectural, historical and hysterical.

In the child's world, a slide is for climbing up, dangling from, pondering over, as well as sliding down — on Yonge Street at Lawrence Avenue.

Above, one man's reaction to Sculpture 67, a mammoth display of contemporary sculpture in Nathan Phillips Square.

On these pages, a museum . . . and a museum piece. Below, the Royal Ontario Museum at the corner of fashionable Bloor Street, the world's largest university museum, with more than a million items displayed.

54

Casa Loma — a castle, not on the
Rhine but on Austin Terrace.
Toronto's most famous landmark is
transformed at Christmastime
into a winter fantasyland for children.

In addition to its imposing facade, Union Station boasts not a few touches of elegance that most travellers never notice. Two of them — the lanterns high over the main concourse, and an intricate mosaic ceiling. Below, budding engineers man a pretend train in the lakeshore park.

57

Toronto's marketplaces are as varied as
its people. Above, the air-conditioned,
heated, soothingly lit, palm-planted
mall at Yorkdale, the world's largest
covered shopping plaza.
Opposite, air-conditioned by open
windows, sunlit, floors paved with
lettuce leaves, St. Lawrence Market,
where shoppers can still pinch, poke,
smell, and sample the merchandise.
On the preceding pages, University
Avenue, looking north toward the
Parliament Buildings, and the re-born
Royal Alexandra Theatre.

On this page, two real-life pieces
of op art — nightlit C.N.E. ferris
wheels and the balconies of the
Inn on the Park.
Opposite, the sparkling colours
of an Impressionist painting
— spring in Edwards Gardens.

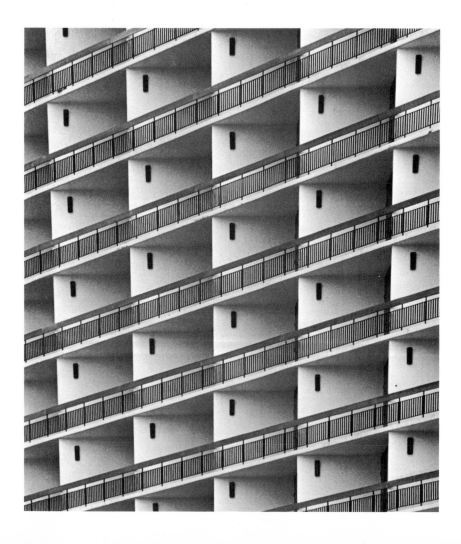

Two popular features of Nathan Phillips Square, the drawn bow of Henry Moore's Archer, *and the skating rink. Opposite, the Art Gallery of Toronto, parking lot packed for a new exhibition.*

Come winter, harbour activity
virtually grinds to a halt,
as piers and breakwater
hibernate beneath a crust of ice.

Commerce and Industry

For the first fifty years of its existence, Toronto was far more of a commercial than an industrial centre. Perhaps this is what gave rise to a resentment of its residents by the rest of the country, an attitude that persists to an extent even today. To the early pioneer, using up his health and strength in the wilderness, it must have seemed unfair that the fruits of his labours and the little cash he ever saw all went to the Town, whose residents knew little or nothing of backbreaking toil, and whose idea of hard work was to sit, pen in hand, crouched over a ledger.

The little settlements were served by small general stores, whose owners for the most part ordered their stock from travellers, many of them coming from Montreal, the centre for overseas markets. Often, when the goods arrived months later, they proved of inferior quality, and the storekeepers found it more satisfactory to deal directly with wholesalers. Since Montreal was far distant, they came to the Toronto warehouses, and the owners found it worthwhile to stock merchandise in both quantity and quality. When the railways came in the 1850's, the traffic in goods increased by leaps and bounds. Wholesalers could import more easily, and deliveries were possible to outlying areas even in the wintertime.

The best stores were to be found on Yonge Street. The Golden Lion, retail house of Robert Walker & Co., stood where the King Edward Hotel was later built. In 1869 Timothy Eaton bought up a dwindling business and built it into a commercial empire. Holt Renfrew, furriers; Birks-Ellis-Ryrie, jewellers; Aikenhead, hardware; Rawlinson, furniture—all built respectable businesses which have lasted to the present. By the turn of the century, there were countless retail outlets in the city, and Jesse Ketchum, whose tanning business was one of a handful of retail establishments in 1812, would have gasped at the growth of competition.

Early Toronto advertising was a far cry from today's multi-million-dollar campaigns. But the combination of discreet promotion and good value for money received began to make the city known as a centre of progressive merchandising. Today Toronto is the advertising capital of Canada.

It was not until the railways came in force in the 1850's that the city developed any great industrial effort. Built on the flats, it lacked even water power of any amount, and a score of smaller settlements were better known for production of local wares than was Toronto.

With the coming of the railways, the population of southern Ontario greatly increased. There was a bigger demand for goods, which could now be more cheaply manufactured in a centre with a supply of low-cost labour and with soft coal readily available for steam power. Toronto, crisscrossed by railways, provided both. Industry grew, bringing prosperity and elegant living for the few, and in its train the gifts of smoke, dirt, and overcrowding.

The Toronto Industrial Exhibition, which first opened in 1879 and was to grow to be the largest annual fair in the world, displayed the possibilities of manufactured articles and factory techniques. Permanent buildings were constructed for the fair,

which have been supplemented and replaced over the years, till now the Canadian National Exhibition attracts over three million visitors annually. The buildings are used by more than forty trade displays during the rest of the year, and in November the Coliseum is the site of the Royal Agricultural Winter Fair, a fitting climax to the fall fairs held in rural communities throughout the country, and one of the largest agricultural fairs in the world. During World War II the Coliseum also served as a barracks for the Air Force.

In the early days of the Exhibition, alert businessmen profited by what they saw on display, and new ideas and methods raised the standard of manufacturing. The protective tariff policies of the government helped stimulate industry, and Toronto as a manufacturing centre was on its way. By the turn of the century electricity began to be used, which cut down the noise and slightly lowered the accident rate — a boon for the families of eight and ten, who lived a block or so away from Father's place of work and depended on his $8 a week for food, shelter, heat, clothing, and future security. This was before the days of Workmen's Compensation and unemployment insurance. When power was brought from Niagara, the rates were cut in half, and manufacturers reaped the benefit. Shipping concerns grew in importance, as the Harbour Commission came into being, and Toronto came to be known as a lake port as well as a railway terminal.

When war broke out, tremendous demands were made on Toronto factories; business boomed; men died, but profits soared. And when hostilities ceased, there was ready money to plough back into the business of reconversion. Despite the Depression and a second world war, the volume of business continues to grow.

The Toronto Board of Trade, begun in 1845, is still the mouthpiece of the industries. Many of the Canadian banks have their headquarters here. The Toronto Stock Exchange, incorporated in 1878, has grown until for a time in the 1950's it showed a greater volume of trading than any other 'Change in the world, including New York's. It is still, despite automation, modern architecture, and blasé sophistication, a place of ill-concealed excitement, where fairy tales come true and fortunes can be made or lost in a day. Scandals discreetly handled, public relations administered professionally, a reasonably select society, it is as natural for the son of a Forest Hill resident to look forward to a seat on the Toronto Exchange as for his wife to covet membership in the Granite Club.

Architecturally, Toronto suffered from the growth of heavy industry. Districts that had once been the centre of elegance and refinement now were coated with oily soot, and even modern vacuums and air conditioning could not cope with the daily output of factory chimneys. People began to use words like air-pollution and smog, while complaints mounted in City Hall. Public health officers quoted statistics on the effects of poor housing and sooty air, and the work of pioneer conservationists like Stuart Chase began to be quoted by intellectuals. Dinner conversation in the '30's included topics that would have made Edwardian hostesses swoon. "Even the Indians," it was repeated,

Since the opening of the St. Lawrence Seaway, Toronto has become more and more an international seaport. Here the ships of three countries lie at anchor in the harbour.

A prominent air-travel centre, Toronto plays host to planes from London, Paris, and even Buttonville. Small private and sightseeing planes are based at Toronto Island Airport.

"knew enough not to drink the water they used for sewage disposal." The general ugliness and inefficiency which resulted from original lack of foresight and later procrastination had at last oozed into public consciousness.

City planning was begun, too late, of course, to be truly effective or anything but exorbitantly expensive, but there was nothing else to do. Even the successful factory owner, while watching closely to see that the graph charts continue the upward curve, must have a place fit to live in, and his wife at home will give him no peace till she gets it. He moves to the suburbs, only to find that there are factories going up a few blocks from his new home. Even he finally recognizes the need for planning.

World War II, although it cost millions, did put an end to the Depression, and there was a resultant wave of prosperity. People had extra money; more important, automation began to provide leisure and there was time to spend looking at one's surroundings. It was a golden era for Causes. Women's committees formed to Save Our Ravines and Save Our Buildings (ugly or not, they are old, and ours!). Cleanup weeks were organized, and the days

before the twenty-fifth of December came to be the time to Put Christ Back in Christmas by floodlighting the front of the house. Toronto at last began to look at itself.

The year 1947 saw the formation of the Toronto and Suburban Planning Board. It also brought the first air pollution bylaw into being. (Forest Hill Village had passed its own law two years before.) Factories began to go up that were not designed as Dickensian workhouses. The doctrine of motion study and the idea that clean, semi-quiet working conditions made for efficiency had come to stay. Some pessimists maintained that it would take a nuclear war to clean up Toronto, but events have proved them wrong. There are still areas of hideous squalor, but in contrast some of the suburban industrial districts, with their landscaped grounds and well-integrated buildings, make an impressive approach to the city. Toronto architects have won awards around the world with their designs for office buildings and factories. The boom seems to be lasting indefinitely, but in spite of the constant presence of bulldozers, piledrivers, and scaffolding, it is a beautiful city that is emerging.

Toronto, the industrial and industrious.
Above, the Toronto-Dominion Centre
under construction, and oil tanks on
Commissioners Street. Below, two views of
the Gardiner Expressway's improbable
curves and chords.

The Oldest Established Annual
Exhibition in the World is another
cherished Toronto tradition, and the
sign that fall has arrived. The
Prince's Gate, at left, was dedicated
by the Prince of Wales in 1927. For
the youngsters, the Midway is an
annual treat to be relished almost as
much as Christmas, and a mother's
patience is put to the test as she
watches her offspring make
the rounds.

Highland regiments have long been a traditional part of Toronto parades. Once headquartered in the old University Avenue Armories, several regiments were displaced, amidst tirades and tears, when the elderly building was razed to make way for the new courthouse, right.

How to use a harbour for pleasure and profit.
Left, a smartly turned out crew receives the salute
in the RCYC regatta sail-past. And a sturdy
lake steamship at anchor, right.
On the preceding pages, St. James' Cathedral's
west entrance, left, and a member of the
North Toronto Hunt Club, on Steeles Avenue.

Where in the hustle and squawk of a large city can one find an oasis of calm? Below, an office worker basks in the noon sun by the City Hall fountain. At right, the Central Library, a gift of Andrew Carnegie, containing some 430,000 titles; far right, a moment of meditation during Remembrance Day services at the Cenotaph in front of the old City Hall.

84

The madding crowd — rush hour at Queen and Yonge Streets.

The Canadian National Exhibition, where the heady mixture of aromas from hot dogs, vinegar, dust, and straw takes Toronto back to its childhood. Here the Midway at midday.

University students, while an integral part of the city, inhabit
a world of their own — particularly in Scarborough College, left,
where the streets are indoors. Below, York University's futuristic
sundial and the more traditional University of Toronto. On this
page, the imposing doors of University College.

Two of the countless houses of worship that have given Toronto the soubriquet, City of Churches. Below, Wexford Presbyterian on Lawrence Avenue in Scarborough. Right, St. John's Lithuanian Lutheran Church on Poplar Plains.

Downtown, uptown, in the suburbs, apartments everywhere and new ones appearing like toadstools every day. On these and the following pages, some of the hundreds of Toronto cliff dwellings: left, Avenue Road; above, Broadway Avenue; right, St. Clair and Walmer Road.

Three views in the
Don Valley Parkway area.

97

The Young City

What do the children and young people do in Toronto?

Children start to school at five years of age, sometimes earlier if a junior kindergarten has been established in their district. Private nursery schools thrive, under license, as in these days of crowded living and no help, many mothers have neither the space nor the energy to cope with lively preschoolers on a full-time basis. There have been kindergartens in Toronto since 1874, and it was the second city in the world to add them to the regular school system. Perhaps the law passed in 1872 forbidding the hiring of children under ten for factory work helped. At any rate, the modern school, with its pastel walls, scientifically designed lighting, bleached wood desks, and composition blackboards, is a long step forward from the schools of the '60's and '70's when one teacher had as many as a hundred pupils in a class, and salaries for women were often less than half that of men. No wonder that truancy was the greatest problem that the School Board had to contend with. Little children of six and seven sat without materials to work with, sometimes lacking slates, and always short of books and copy paper, from nine till four. They learned by rote and recited their lessons in a chorus, with corporal punishment the fate of anyone who spoke out of turn, wriggled, or in any way drew attention to himself. There were few desks, and the younger pupils were set on benches, too high to let their feet touch the floor. The teachers were ill-trained, overworked, despised by the more affluent members of the community, and hated cordially by the more intelligent children, who blamed them for the frustration and boredom which were the result of the system.

But not all the teachers were helpless misfits, and not all board members self-interested politicians. Many of the leading educationalists were as appalled at the situation as we might be today. There were men like Ryerson, who fought for free schools and served as Superintendent of Education for thirty-two years; like Jesse Ketchum, deprived of schooling in his own youth and determined that no child should be similarly handicapped as long as he could prevent it; Brown, McMurrich, Ogden, able and persuasive. There was Miss Hester How, given the unenviable job of teaching the first class of delinquent boys in the Ward, and making such a success of the job that the school was a pioneer in such areas as public health services, guidance, fresh-air camps, day nurseries, and Juvenile Court. Today's children, if they recognize these names at all, know them perhaps as the names of schools, and may never realize the debt they owe to the people who once answered to them. Most children are eager to start kindergarten and grade one, and stay in school till they are sixteen, which is the legal age for leaving. Many continue on to finish high school, and never realize that till 1921 it cost money to attend school after grade eight, and that for thousands of young people, a high school diploma was an idle

*On the preceding page, the Island
lagoon, a refuge for romantics as well
as practical boat fanciers. Above, the new
Frost Building echoes the circle of
Queen's Park. Opposite, the expanding
University of Toronto campus . . .
the clock tower of Sir Daniel Wilson
residence, and at left, Sydney Smith Hall.*

dream. Now vocational and commercial schools train students in
a tremendous variety of trades, while scholarships and bursaries
are available to help hundreds through university. The days of
the Family Compact, when education was for the privileged few,
are indeed gone forever.

When school is out, what then? Chopping wood, fetching coke
in a sack from the gas company's yard, selling newspapers,
running a bootblack stand — these occupations of past days are
gone. Some youngsters have paper routes, but even part-time
delivery boys must be over fourteen. Vacant lots to play in are
scarce, fast-moving traffic makes the streets unsafe, and cracker-
box apartments offer no outlet for childish energy. Today's
children are accused of being indulged, pampered, and lacking
initiative, but the critics seldom allow for the chronic lack of
space which prohibits any but the most organized spending of
leisure time.

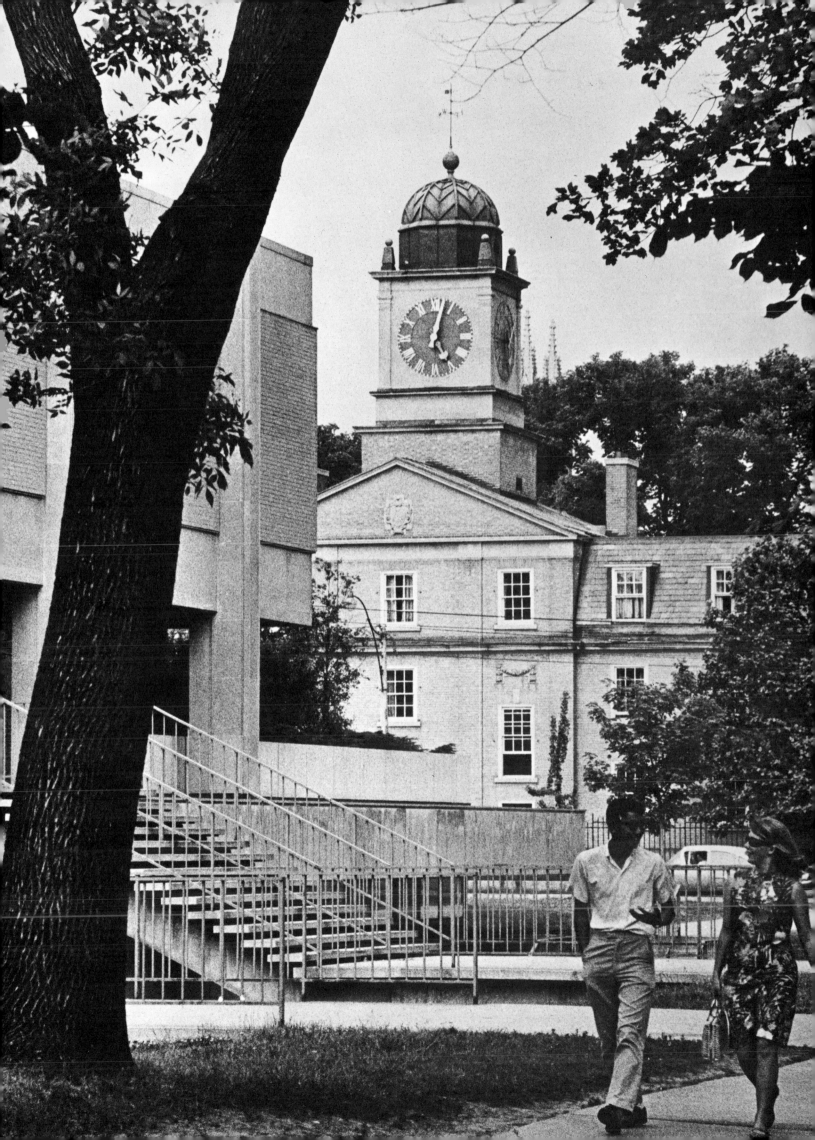

Saturday night is Hockey Night in Canada, especially in Toronto. Above, traffic snarls and fans jostle one another for a place in line and a chance at last-minute tickets at Maple Leaf Gardens. Right, Canada's National Passion. The game stops for a breath-holding split-second when a goal is scored. On the following pages, two more popular attractions: the Royal Winter Fair, and the Metro Police Games.

Churches and service clubs have stepped into the breach. There are sports programs run by the "Y", Boy Scouts, Girl Guides, supervised playgrounds, and countless after-school activities. Volunteer adults referee baseball and hockey matches; the essential suburban accessory, the car, is used to ferry players back and forth across the city for practices and scheduled games. The car pool is in use, too, for music lessons, dancing lessons, dramatic classes, or hours in conversational French. Certainly the young children seem to be over-organized, but how else can you keep them occupied in a big city, where aimless wandering or time to think, the ancient prerogatives of childhood, can only lead to trouble?

The teenagers work. They work at school (and the courses grow more demanding every year), they work after school in a variety of jobs, and in the summer months it is the exception who is not employed. They have their own agency, where registered names are on tap for interested employers, and young people can be hired at a reasonable salary for such jobs as filing, typing, babysitting, youth leadership, manual labour, and a hundred other occupations. It is the fashion to have a job, and the money earned will buy clothes or a car, pay for recreation, or may be saved towards university fees.

More and more of these teenagers realize that a degree is a necessity in their chosen occupations. Besides, their horizons have been enlarged by the influence of libraries, museums, art galleries, and concerts, all employed fully in conjunction with schoolwork, and television is still a cultural force in most homes.

They want to learn more. They want to go to university. High school dropout rates are still high, as they are all over the country, and newspapers play up the delinquency figures, but the majority of young people in the city are sober and practical.

Even Bishop Strachan might approve of their ideals. He fought the establishment of Kings College for sixteen years, till he could be assured that it would be under the control of the Anglican Church (even though the Church of England was never established legally in Upper Canada). When it was freed of religious domination in 1849, he flew off to England and raised money to build his own college, Trinity. Not till 1887 was federation adopted, and Trinity, University College, St. Michael's (Catholic), Victoria (Methodist), and eventually Wycliffe and Knox made up the University of Toronto. Women were admitted first in 1884, and now the college grounds are crowded winter and summer, day and night, with extension courses drawing in thousands of "off-campus" students, who work late hours towards a degree that may mean security or promotion in their daily jobs.

The new universities are offering experiments in their courses. The money that is poured into equipment in high schools, public schools, and universities serves as an investment in adult education. Night classes are held in almost all the large schools, while the auditoriums, swimming pools, and gymnasiums double as community centres for recreation and culture. There is no lack of facilities for the young person in Toronto, if he has the desire to seek them out. And if they prove inadequate, as they sometimes do, if he can only find purpose and excitement in his life by rebelling against society, is it the fault of the city? Is there, perhaps, a lack of response to the challenge of living within the individual himself? Finding the answer to this may well prove to be one of the greatest problems any big city will have to answer in the next twenty-five years.

*Aficionados of all forms of racing haven't far
to go to find action. There's car racing at Mosport,
stock cars at Pinecrest, thoroughbred racing
at Woodbine and Greenwood.*

At the Royal York Hotel, painted muses look down this evening on an exhibition of an age-old art — the somewhat esoteric, very personal art of coiffure. Right, spray in the setting sun adds just the touch of drama that a swan's portrait deserves. One of the more dignified inhabitants of High Park.

Saturday night, at the Friars . . .   *and Sunday morning, at St. James'.*

The New Torontonian

Since the Second World War, the upswing of immigration has brought thousands of new Canadians to live in Toronto. This one change has perhaps done more than anything else in the past hundred years to alter the character of the city. It is not uncommon to hear as many as seven different languages spoken on one trip in a bus or subway. Whole areas that were once depressingly Anglo-Saxon in their respectable poverty now burst with the type of life that only comes from a heterogeneous mixture of cultures. Latin, Celt, Slav, Balkan, Greek, Scandinavian, Teutonic — all these races and more have brought Toronto a colour and cosmopolitan flavour she never knew before. Once a Torontonian's idea of a night out consisted of dinner and dancing at one of the few big hotels. Now he can choose from a host of restaurants, each with its own national cuisine, and afterwards attend a film or play in any of four or five languages. Before World War II visiting Chinatown was a novelty for the brave and daring. Now Chinese food comes in pre-frozen packages in the supermarket, and such words as pizza, espresso, blintzes, and smörgasbord are an integral part of the housewife's vocabulary.

The streets are different, too. Graceful Indian women in gaily coloured saris hurry across the university grounds, their feet shod in most uncharacteristic but practical snow boots. Bearded intellectuals rate scarcely a second glance, and daring fashions, displayed in the discreetly expensive shopping mews are no more extreme than those modelled by onlookers. Yet all is not changed. The Methodist background is still reflected in the uncompromising, sensible shoes and black carry-all of the determined bargain hunter, braving the crowds for the downtown January sales. Young secretaries may sip coffee in the gaily striped chairs of a chi-chi sidewalk café, but they still do it with an air of determined enjoyment, as though expecting criticism. Their bosses have learned to tolerate birth control pills on the office desks, hair styles that lengthen coffee breaks by ten minutes, and yearly maternity leaves, but they still rely on the Businessman's Special in the exclusively male corner of the local restaurant, where the menu is as predictable as the company and the conversation.

It takes more than three or four generations to develop that certain something in a city that gives it a personality. Toronto is gradually changing, from a centre of puritanical boredom to a growing city of ideas. Visitors pour in, every day of the year, some for business, some for pleasure. What does the city have to offer them?

In fine weather, the parks are full. Most of these were lands donated to the city; High Park in the west, Allan Gardens where the first fireworks displays were held in 1875, and Riverdale, which includes the zoo. Eglinton Park was a brickyard till the clay ran out. The subway yards now stand on another abandoned clay deposit, once the site of the Davis pottery works. Toronto Island, now reclaimed for park use and banned to industry, is also noted as the site of the Island School, where hundreds of children each year have the experience of living in a country setting for part of a week, studying natural science at first hand.

After the Second World War, the state of the parks was deplorable, and despite the prevalence of old and beautiful trees, Toronto had a lower percentage of green areas than almost any other large city on the continent. The establishment of the Metro Conservation Authority in 1954 helped to draw public attention to the importance of park land, not only as recreational asset, but for flood control. Thanks to this body, Edwards Gardens in North York and James Gardens in Etobicoke have been developed. The Authority is continually fighting for permanent green areas against the advance of industry and high-rise apartments. It argues that parks are a more valuable legacy to hand on to the next generations than concrete and plate glass, the two icons of modern living.

There is lots to see in Toronto now. The Royal Ontario Museum attracts scholars and visitors from around the world. The Art Gallery is always open, and many smaller galleries throughout the city specialize in different types of exhibition. At one time, the downtown residents might have been dependent on such amusements as lantern slide showings in the grounds of the Metropolitan Church on fine summer evenings, or a band concert in Queen's Park. Now there are at least a dozen free attractions in libraries, galleries, theatre lobbies, and public buildings, any day of the month.

"Meet me at the fountain," a time-honoured Toronto meeting place. Four or five generations have made their rendezvous here, at the quiet end of the Ex, the Canadian National Exhibition. A stiff walk from the razzmatazz of the Midway, the Horticultural Building lifts its Victorian cupola against a brilliant Exhibition-weather sky. Upholding another tradition, dressed in the uniform of the original defenders, youthful Torontonians drill at Fort York, and for one bright afternoon time slips back a century and a half.

Only a colour photograph could do justice
to the riotous hues of the C.N.E. midway
and the discreet splashes of colour on
University Avenue, looking north to the
Parliament Buildings.

In the 1830's, meetings held in North Toronto were scheduled for nights near the full of the moon, to help members find their way to and fro through the mud. Those early residents would be amazed at the present parade of traffic that makes seven to eight p.m. another rush hour, as citizens hurry out to their evening engagements, social, cultural, or educational. Theatres offer everything from Greek tragedy to the latest "Absurd" effort from London or New York. There are only two good theatres for use by road companies, but this lack is overshadowed by the development of local professional groups. Little theatres, some with miniature stages, or platforms for productions in the round, spring up on every side. New York producers have learned to be wary of Toronto audiences. Perhaps the attitude comes as a legacy from the thrifty pioneer ancestry and generations of disapproval of any theatrical goings-on, but theatregoers have a way of rejecting the second rate that is brought to them, despite advance publicity and the glamour of Broadway. On the other hand, this is a ballet town, and audiences welcome hysterically companies that rate only lukewarm praise in other centres. In the days before moving pictures, Toronto supported many legitimate houses. The Theatre Royal was the first, opened in 1848, and the Lyric at Bay and Dundas welcomed such stars as David Kessler and Jacob Adler, who were to bring the Yiddish theatre such fame. For lower tastes, there were the Star and the Gaiety, where burlesque attracted the customers. St. Lawrence Hall, built in 1851, knew such famous names as Patti and Jenny Lind. Massey Hall, built in the '90's, is still rated acoustically as one of the finest in the world. There always seems to have been theatrical activity of some sort going on, since the earliest amateur performances by the military personnel in the York garrison. Now television has its English-language headquarters in Toronto, and acting is accepted as a profession, even by the income tax department.

Toronto has been known for years as a City of Churches. "Toronto the Good" was a common sneer in past years, though the speakers were seldom aware of the districts which compared in sordid romance with the seamier sides of New York, Chicago, or a dozen other big towns. The centre of the Toronto diocese, St. James' Cathedral, is the third of its name to stand on that site, the others having been destroyed by fire. Holy Trinity, which stands behind Eaton's, was opened in 1847, with the stipulation that the pews should always be kept free. Methodists began corporate worship in 1818, Roman Catholics in 1828, Presbyterians in 1831. These denominations are well represented today, as are Baptists, Lutherans, Jews, Christian Scientists, and many smaller sects including Buddhism and other religions from the East. Churchgoing is still a weekly pastime in Toronto.

Visitors can shop in any number of department stores or at shopping plazas, complete with noontime theatres, art exhibits, fountains, indoor gardens, and restaurants. There are open-air markets, too, in some of the ethnic areas where bits of Europe seem strangely transplanted. Deliveries, which once would have been made by sleigh or horse-drawn cart, are now in the hands of brisk teenagers, whose driving habits can cause suburban housewives pangs of anxiety for the safety of their offspring.

Should the visitor be lost, he can count on help from a policeman on the corner, still a familiar figure, though the uniform has changed from the days when a cry of, "Here comes Uncle," sent young boys scattering from illegal street ballgames. Should he want the news of the day, he can have his choice of newspapers, some published in the city and some imported from half a dozen countries, in as many foreign tongues. Television is to be had in any hotel room; canned music plays in most supermarkets, dentists' offices, or undertaking parlours. Indeed if he wants silence, he may have to retreat to the nearest public library, and even there his neighbour may have a small transistor radio up his sleeve, bleating tunes that are the choice of one of the local radio stations.

He will find, perhaps, that outdoor entertainment is not as zestful as it used to be. Public hangings have been discontinued since 1869, and elections and Twelfth of July parades lack some of the more active participation that used to send victims home with broken heads. Parades are well-run, orderly affairs, with police directing traffic, newsreel cameras carefully placed, and for those who prefer to stay at home, television commentators to describe the proceedings in words of one syllable, with faces masked in professional charm. There is still the occasional fire, but little danger of the disaster of 1904, when the warehouse district burned merrily for two weeks. Crises are more likely to come from severe storms, or a power failure, when modern conveniences stop dead and mechanized citizens find themselves almost helpless.

When the time comes to leave the city, there are planes to catch out at the International Airport, or trains leaving from Union Station, a junction point for the whole of Canada. Perhaps our visitor will depart by ship, now that Toronto is an ocean port, via the Seaway. If he drives, super-highways are available, travelling north, east, or west. And as he leaves, by car, plane, bus, or train, what will he take with him as a memory of Toronto? What can anyone take of a big city? Sights, smells, sounds — or perhaps that uncanny combination of all three which is what we call atmosphere.

As in the rest of Canada, the tide of immigrants flowing into Toronto has resulted, not in a melting pot, but in an ethnic patchwork across the city and a distinctly cosmopolitan air to our parks. Here, High Park on a sunny Saturday.

The tired buff clapboard of
Malton Airport has been
replaced by a gleaming cube
of concrete and steel, visible
for miles . . . Toronto
International Airport.

122

One of the few surviving
Lancasters is preserved on
Toronto's lakefront, to the
gratitude of sentimental World
War II airmen. Happily,
the airship remains aloft, if
only by a few feet.

Park-strolling is a favourite
Sunday pastime, especially
among Torontonians of
European origin. On the
Island, above, or on the city-
side shore, you can wander for
hours without hearing a word of
English. Opposite, a solitary
pensioner on the banks of
the Island lagoon.
On the preceding pages,
Toronto at dusk and the
pageantry accompanying the
opening of the Provincial
Parliament, Queen's Park.

Whatever the weather . . .

. . . Torontonians make the best of it.

Terpsichore has many guises, and all have their
Toronto devotees . . .

the body beautiful . . .

in the Pavlova tradition, Joan Killoran and
Gilbert Rome of the National Ballet . . .

. . . nimble natives.

On the page preceding,
the East Block of the
Parliament Buildings.

Rose, heliotrope,
aquamarine . . . the
founder of Ontario
Hydro stands on
his stone spillway,
solemnly watching some
of the more frivolous
results of his great fiscal
achievement.
University Avenue,
looking south, with the
lights of the
Toronto-Dominion
Centre at the top left.
And here, the Colonnade
— forty-nine shops,
two and a half
restaurants, and elegant
apartment living.

137

The now legendary fence at
Osgoode Hall, left, still highly
effective in protecting the grounds
from meandering cows.
Above, yet another village-
within-a-city, Markham Village,
of special interest to lovers of
art and antiques.

High rise . . . the architectural byword of the sixties. And it's also the best way to view Riverdale Zoo, below.

Oblivious to the rush-hour traffic,
on University Avenue, left,
Sir John A. Macdonald eyes Sir Adam Beck.
At the O'Keefe Centre, below, the
parade of international performers has
given Toronto a heightened glamour and
turned it into an entertainment capital.

143

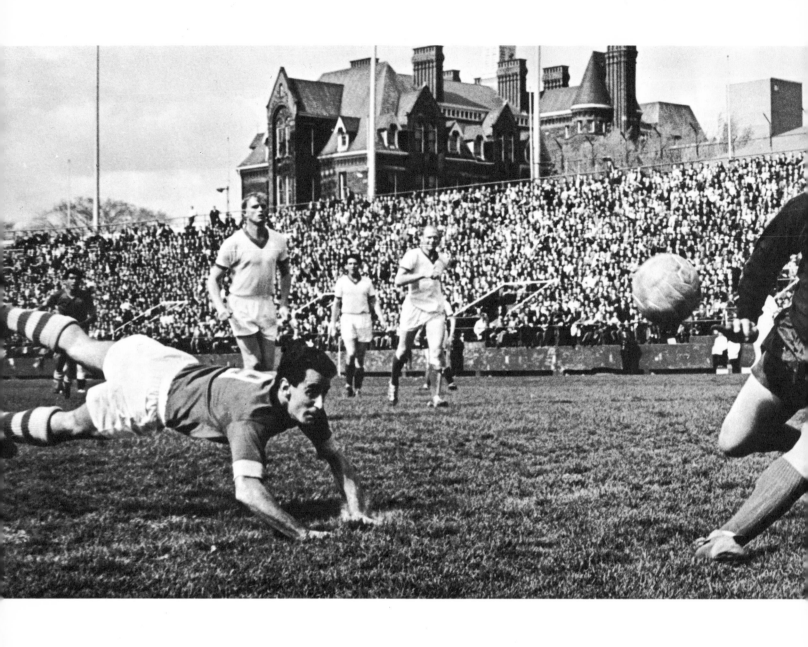

The variety of sports here is another reflection of the diverse ethnic origins of Toronto's people . . . soccer from the central Europeans (at Varsity Stadium), curling from the Scots, and our own brand of football (at C.N.E. Stadium).

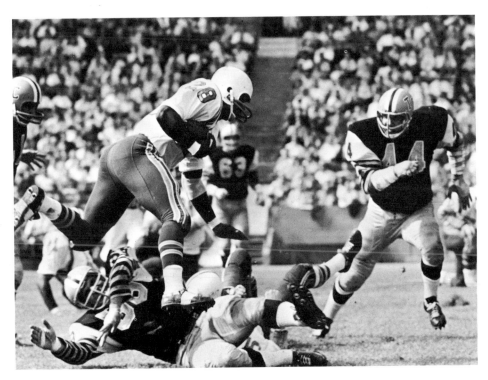

*St. Lawrence Market again
— a tang of garlic, scent
of freshly butchered beef.*

*Winter — a time of frivolity and, on the following
pages, breathtaking beauty and grim determination.*

*Twilight on the Macdonald-Cartier Freeway, left, at Kennedy Road,
and sunlight on a wrought-iron railing, St. Clair Avenue and Walmer Road.*

153

Colour and Lithography   Litho-Print Limited